WINCHESTER

FAKE IT 'TIL YOU MAKE IT

KA 0440786 5

Bryony Kimmings and Tim Grayburn

FAKE IT 'TIL YOU MAKE IT

OBERON BOOKS
LONDON

WWW.OBERONBOOKS.COM

UNIVERSITY OF WINCHESTER
LIBRARY

First published in 2015 by Oberon Books Ltd
521 Caledonian Road, London N7 9RH
Tel: +44 (0) 20 7607 3637 / Fax: +44 (0) 20 7607 3629
e-mail: info@oberonbooks.com
www.oberonbooks.com

Copyright © Bryony Kimmings and Tim Grayburn, 2015

Foreword © James Leadbitter, 2015; *Foreword* © Georgie Harman,
2015; *Bird Hunter, Matador, Shaman, Bride* © Andy Field, 2015

Reprinted with revisions in 2015

Bryony Kimmings and Tim Grayburn are hereby identified
as authors of this play in accordance with section 77 of the
Copyright, Designs and Patents Act 1988. The authors have
asserted their moral rights.

All rights whatsoever in this play are strictly reserved and
application for performance etc. should be made before
commencement of rehearsal to Avalon, 4a Exmoor Street,
London, UK, W10 6BD. No performance may be given unless
a licence has been obtained, and no alterations may be made in
the title or the text of the play without the author's prior written
consent.

You may not copy, store, distribute, transmit, reproduce or
otherwise make available this publication (or any part of it) in
any form, or binding or by any means (print, electronic, digital,
optical, mechanical, photocopying, recording or otherwise),
without the prior written permission of the publisher. Any person
who does any unauthorized act in relation to this publication may
be liable to criminal prosecution and civil claims for damages.

A catalogue record for this book is available from the British
Library.

PB ISBN: 9781783199518
E ISBN: 9781783199525

Cover and image photography by Richard Davenport

Printed and bound by Marston Book Services, Didcot.
eBook conversion by CPI Group (UK) Ltd, Croydon, CR0 4YY.

Visit www.oberonbooks.com to read more about all our books
and to buy them. You will also find features, author interviews and
news of any author events, and you can sign up for e-newsletters
so that you're always first to hear about our new releases.

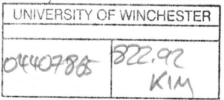

UNIVERSITY OF WINCHESTER

0440788   822.92
          KIM

Foreword

I'm halfway through watching *Fake It 'Til You Make It* and one question is bothering me. Where is Tim's voice? Then, as if Bryony and Tim know what I am thinking, Tim takes off his mask, comes to the microphone and speaks. I realize this wait was intentional and that my need for him to speak has to be balanced with his need to feel confident with what he is about to do. Tim speaks from the heart, he holds his hands to hide his nerves, he takes a hammer to his own and society's taboos. It's a beautiful moment. I feel connected to him, like I know what he's going through and why he's doing it.

There was a moment in 2010 that has stuck with me, that I have to remind myself of now and again. I'd been told by my social worker that my application for homeless status had been rejected by Hackney Council, that I would be kicked out of the homeless hostel, leaving me with nowhere to live – a feat of such stupid logic it would make Monty Python proud. Later that week I see my therapist, and she asks me about my lack of anger. 'It was a nightmare last time, so I'm kind of used to it.'

'You've been homeless before?' she asks. As so many times before, I retell my story of coming out of a year long admission in 2000 and how long it took to get the Bed and Breakfast accommodation from Barnet Council, in a distant and matter of fact way.

'Y'know most people haven't been homeless James, they haven't spent long periods in mental health hospitals, they haven't made serious suicide attempts. I'm wondering what it would be like for you if you didn't see these things as normal. What if you saw them in a different way? Could we explore that?' It was such a therapist thing to say, and annoyingly, she was bloody right.

It hits me in the gut on my way home. Luckily, I've got my sun glasses with me, so my crying on public transport can be undertaken more subtly.

A week later I go for my Employment and Support Allowance (Disability Benefits) assessment by ATOS to find out if the government thinks I'm fit for work. The 'Doctor' asks me if I can bend over, walk down the street and use a telephone. I explain

I don't have a physical condition, I have multiple mental health diagnoses. He doesn't seem interested, empathetic or even to have heard of my main diagnosis. I cycle home feeling dirty, like I've done something wrong, like it's my fault. I hate myself for being in this situation. I am weak, flawed, a piece of shit.

With her arms around me, the snot and tears flowing off my chin, my partner says 'I'm sorry, you shouldn't be treated like this, it's horrific.' I can see the anger in her eyes, the red mist descending. I wonder why I don't feel angry; am I internalizing the failings of an intentionally broken welfare system in ways I hadn't realized? The answer is obviously yes, but being able to change that is going to take time and dedication.

It's September 2013, I'm in Riga, Latvia at a festival called Homo Novus, it's the first time I've been able work outside of the UK in four years. Getting here was an achievement and involved 16 mg of Valium for a three hour flight. I'm here to present the finished version of a autobiographical performance called *Mental*, in which I weave a narrative of medical records and police files against my version of the battles with mental distress and police repression I've lived through. It's taken about two years to make, and that hasn't been that pleasant. OK, that's an understatement. Normally I like making art, but this process has involved reliving trauma, a hospital admission, disagreements, and a large amount of medication. I've done the set up, I know what I'm going to say and the order in which to show things but I'm wondering what I'm doing. Why am I doing this? What are the positives? What will people think of me?

I've agreed to do four performances, which after the first two seems like a bad idea, my body is aching, I want to punch myself and I feel ultra paranoid. I've just shown fifty complete strangers my intimate medical records, which include details of acute mental distress, suicide attempts and the thoughts of a Freudian therapist which can be described at best as culturally and socially backward, and at worst as progressive as Mumford and Son's best work – and yes Mumford and Sons and best work is an oxymoron.

Now, I'm used to taking risks in making art, I've broken laws, bled, been beaten by the police, spied on by E.ON, censored

by Starbucks and walked a fine line between life and death. I'm not saying this to sound 'hard' or 'manly'; I think most art is not really prepared to break taboos – so it's important I practise what I preach. Yet there is something about performing the *Mental* piece that feels harder than anything I've done. It's odd – because all I'm really doing is sitting in a bed, telling a story, showing the reports the state holds about me and playing some records. I am, though, nailing my flag to the mast. I'm outing myself as mad and the reality of that isn't always pretty. The stigma people with mental illnesses face is still massive and it would be perfectly sensible to want to avoid this discrimination by hiding my illness.

It's post second performance in Riga and I want to go home. I think the show is going down like a lead balloon. I think people are giving me funny looks, no one has spoken to me about the show, either to bitch or complement. Then like that moment during my therapy session three years early something happens that sticks with me, that I always remind myself of when I'm doubtful about the quality of *Mental.* Someone approaches me, they ask if we can talk. I'm OK with that. They are young and shy. They say 'I've never told anyone this…*pause.* I came to see your piece *Mental.*' I say 'Thank you for coming to see it'. 'I've been seeing a psychiatrist for two years, and no one knows, but I'm not ashamed anymore. I live with my parents and I'm going home to tell them. I think I'm going to tell my best friend.'

I don't know what to say. Saying 'that's great' would be weird, saying 'you're brave', well I hate it when people say that to me, it's not brave – it's just dealing with a reality millions of people live through everyday. Saying anything with words feels incomplete. I'm not a poet, a wordsmith, a writer – I'm really dyslexic, and words are hard for me. I get the feeling I need to say something.

'I'm really pleased you shared that with me, I was about to go and ask the curator to book me an early flight home. I'm not feeling great about this show, the piece whatever this thing is, but… That, what you just said, it means a lot to me. I can't tell you, I'm not good with words.' They smile at me, and I smile back. I think to myself – I don't need to do this show again, my job is done but I also understand that this is why I'm doing it.

Two years later. I'm still touring *Mental.* Not everyone likes it, and that's fine. Mental health isn't something we are all able to engage with – yet. Some people say it's too real. Some people say it's like self harm, some people cry, and some people laugh. Some people give it a one star review and some people five. Luckily I personally don't think it's my job to be liked or loved – I'm an artist, not a pop star or a politician. Like Tim and Bryony, my job is to ask the questions that need asking, see the things that go unseen and break those taboos that need breaking, or try at least.

The mask comes off to reveal Tim, stood stage right in a spotlight, which is both a metaphor and what actually happens in the show. He speaks about being a man, and how he worries about how being open would make him less of one. He speaks of the hope that he has found in both understanding his experience of depression and speaking openly about it. I feel the solidarity in his act, the strength and agency he has found, and the strength and agency he gifts to me. Depression can feel brutally isolating, yet the act of reaching out and being touched is a vital tool to break down the stigma, but also to build mutual support. As Bob Hoskins says in the old BT adverts 'It's good to talk'.

James Leadbitter

Foreword

I'll never forget seeing the play *Fake It 'Til You Make It* at the lovely Theatre Works in St Kilda, a beachside suburb in Melbourne, Australia.

I didn't know what to expect. It was hilarious. I cried my eyes out.

Tim and Bryony's story is deeply personal and absolutely unique to them, but there are many elements of their story that would be part of so many other lives too.

Depression and anxiety are common and don't discriminate: In Australia they affect three million of us a year. Seven Australians die by suicide every day – double the number of people killed on our roads – and five of them will be men. Every person's mental health struggles, every suicide, has a ripple effect on partners, lovers, families, mates and work colleagues.

The prevalence of depression and anxiety is similar in the UK. In any year, nearly one person in five in England has depression, anxiety or both. The suicide rate in the UK is slightly higher than Australia, and because the population in the UK is larger, this equates to seventeen people dying by suicide every day.

In the fifteen years *beyondblue* has been working in Australia, we've increased understanding of and action on these conditions. We now work actively to prevent suicide. Australians are starting to understand that mental health problems touch every family, every workplace and every group of friends. We realize that if we don't have good mental health, everything is compromised. We've come a long way in raising awareness, increasing action and breaking down stigma and discrimination.

However, while most of us now screen for and act early on breast or bowel cancer, high blood pressure or diabetes, still only half identify mental health issues early and seek the support and treatment which will aid recovery and keep work, relationships and quality of life intact.

beyondblue does a great deal of work with men. We know that it is incredibly common for them to internalize their mental health issues, ignore and mask the signs and symptoms, and be embarrassed to admit they're struggling.

Our core message is that strong men take action and ask for help. Strong men talk about their feelings with other strong men, their partner, and their doctor. Just as Tim did.

Our work reaches out not only to men, but to the people who love them, who may not realize what that person is experiencing, or fail to understand the reasons why they might struggle to be open and honest about what they are feeling.

I know many partners have been in Bryony's situation. Faced with a revelation, either willingly or in Tim's case unwillingly, of a 'secret' mental illness, loved ones feel helpless and search for answers. This is so perfectly encapsulated in Bryony's reaction, as she asks 'How do I rescue you?'

What Bryony and Tim discover is that it's not that simple and there is no 'quick fix' to 'rescue' someone from mental illness. Through real-life recordings of intimate conversations, we hear their raw emotions and feelings as they face Tim's illness together.

We do have a clear understanding of why people feel pressured to hide their illnesses. We regularly survey the Australian community to track awareness, attitudes and behaviour surrounding depression and anxiety. While attitudes have improved significantly since the first survey in 2004, it is deeply concerning that in 2012, 29 per cent of respondents said they wouldn't be happy for a person with depression or anxiety to marry into their family. On average, one in seven people also said they believe those with severe depression are weak-willed and one in four believes they should just 'pull themselves together'.

I think you'll find that Tim is neither 'weak-willed' or needs to 'snap out of it'. And I reckon he'd be a catch for any family.

These findings are evidence that stigma and discrimination are stubbornly present. And let's not forget that the definition of stigma is a stain on one's character.

Mental illness has nothing to do with Tim's character – any more than diabetes or skin cancer has. And mental illness can be just as life threatening.

More and more we must understand we need to look after body, mind and spirit. Organizations like *beyondblue* can lay out the facts, influence and support, but there is nothing more powerful than when people speak up and put talent, creativity

and raw honesty into the mix. Tim and Bryony's story cuts through because it's funny, sad, breaks your heart and then lifts you up again.

Their generosity of wanting to start a social movement, to protect others, to show that no one should try to hide what's happening to them – and that it will be OK – is inspiring.

Tim now embraces and manages his condition. Bryony supports him to do so. They are honest in saying it's not easy, but Tim's condition is now part of who they are and what they will be as a family when their baby comes along.

For anyone who has seen the play or who reads this book, you may want to help or get involved. In Australia, we encourage people to visit our website www.beyondblue.org.au to learn more about how you can help someone who is struggling or at risk of suicide and to get involved with *beyondblue.*

Check in with your loved ones today, ask each other how you're doing, and be honest if you are struggling. As Tim and Bryony have shown us, if we understand mental health problems can happen to any of us, and if we embrace them and support each other, we fly.

You are in for a treat.

Georgie Harman
CEO *beyondblue*

Bird Hunter, Matador, Shaman, Bride

1 THE BRYONY-NESS OF BRYONY KIMMINGS

I am trying to think about the Bryony-ness of Bryony Kimmings. I have decided I want to write about a distinctive and perhaps slightly intangible quality that all her work seems to have – a muscular dynamism, a technicolour vividness, an aura of something, a certain kind of charm maybe, a thing, a Bryony thing, a Bryony-ness. What is the Bryony-ness of Bryony Kimmings? What is this elusive component that so compellingly animates her work? It is not just charisma, it is more profound and more artful; something more calculated. I want to try and describe it but I am struggling. I am trying to pull myself from vagueness and cliché towards a more precise description of what makes Bryony's work so interesting and so popular but I keep finding myself back again at the Bryony-ness.

Part of the difficulty I think is that memory is failing me. I have seen at least one version of every piece Bryony has made since I first saw *Sex Idiot* in a small and very crowded room at the Edinburgh Festival in 2010. I have seen some of those pieces a number of times or in a number of incarnations, but despite or perhaps because of this when I try and picture these shows the images are a disordered mess. A riot of cartoon costumes and machine washable fabrics. A mess of old songs and new songs. A carnival of faces from the ridiculous to the heartbreaking. Moments of casual spontaneity and elegant craft. Stories real and imagined.

2 FAIRY TALES

Perhaps part of the reason for this confusion is that a certain slipperiness of images and of meaning is an essential part of the Bryony-ness that I'm trying to describe.

Like fairy tales, Bryony's shows are full of things that are constantly becoming other things. A science experiment that turns into a rave. A confession that turns into a pop song. Props that are first one thing and then another. A bouquet of flowers that transforms into a weapon. A bowl full of pubic hair that becomes a moustache. And always at the centre of all of this confusion is Bryony herself – cycling through a spectacular and seemingly infinite parade of costume changes; bird hunter, matador, shaman, bride, scientist, drunk clown, tropical princess. A carnival of transformations that reached its apotheosis in *Credible Likeable Superstar Role Model* when she transformed into a different person entirely – a curly-haired palaeontologist pop star called Catherine Bennett. Even the nominally 'real' 'non-performers' who have been Bryony's collaborators on her two most recent shows are not there to present any straightforward version of themselves – they too become unreal creatures, costumed fantasies, components in an elaborate imaginary syntax.

Whilst autobiography might provide the basis for Bryony's work it is the way in which those real stories become part of a dynamic, symbolic landscape that sets it apart. A rich, invented world composed in colours, costumes, songs, objects and images; a fairytale realm of contested meanings and metamorphoses.

3 MYTHOLOGIES

What is it that is going on in the vivid imaginary world conjured by one of Bryony's shows?

In *Mythologies*, Roland Barthes describes the process of contemporary mythmaking as a series of appropriations. Stories and images are emptied of the meaning that they once had and are instead employed to consolidate a particular idea – a myth, a story about the way the world is.

I think of Bryony's shows as a similar if perhaps more benign form of mythologizing in which a constellation of signs – a speculum, a story about a sexually transmitted disease, a Spanish bullfighter, woman in a bridal gown, a list of words for a woman's genitals – are co-opted to create a distinct new cosmogony. A new fable, nourished by the resonance of these contradictory references now employed to speak to or speak about something else; something beyond the limits of their earlier meanings. As such the show might be understood not as a story, or at least not the relatively neat relatively linear story the show blurb might suggest, but rather an accumulation of very small stories employed to express a larger idea with a rare richness and complexity.

Perhaps this is the Bryony-ness of Bryony. The ability to make one or two people on a relatively bare stage appear to be components in an elaborate symphony of voices. The quality of making from a few thin splinters of reality a self-contained universe that appears profound in its relevance and positively mythic in scale.

4 DREAMS

Here then is an imaginary world as dense and messy as life itself, and as the doors of the theatre open we are tossed into it. Dressed in feathers or silver foil or pink fairy princess taffeta Bryony reels across the stage, waving cartoon props, pulling silly faces and telling us about abjection and addiction and mental illness, a put-upon ringmaster in some ecstatic circus.

It is like a dream this world. Not in the sense that it is slow or hypnotic or surreal or any of the other things we too-readily associate with dreams. It is like a dream in that it is as vivid and sensual and pregnant with possible meanings as the experience of dreaming; propelled, like any dream, by some delirious internal logic we can't quite figure out even once we've left the auditorium.

Freud described dreaming as a means of thinking by experiencing, suggesting we attach 'complete belief to the hallucinations' and it is only later that we recognize that we have not been experiencing anything at all, only 'thinking in a peculiar way'. Perhaps the same is true of our journey through Bryony's hallucinatory fables. We watch and listen to this dazzlingly entertaining procession of costumes and confessions and as we try and place these disparate pieces together we are thinking by experiencing, exploring ideas made of bodies and melodies and headdresses. Figuring something out in a way that simply wouldn't be possible with words alone.

Andy Field

The story of Bryony and Tim

Originally written by the duo for The New Review
(Part of the *Independent* Sunday supplement)

BRYONY'S STORY

My name is Bryony Kimmings, I am a performance artist from London. I met Tim in June 2013. I had been snaffled away in a massive country house in the Yorkshire Dales for weeks desperately making a show for Edinburgh. Walks, healthy food and long days of writing, going a little stir crazy.

I found myself back in London on a boiling hot weekend. I felt like a new butterfly. My friend was working a local bar and so me and my ladies went out to drink gin. By 10pm Lindsey, my designated winglady, was engrossed with a man called Joe and I was dancing. I remember screeching at Joe that he needed to find someone for me to have sex with. He fired out a text and along came Tim. All freckles and tan. He must have thought I was bonkers.

He says he fancied me the moment he saw me, I can't remember much more than us all dancing down Kingsland road. When I woke up the next morning I realized I had struck gold. Tim was such a gent and had the most gorgeous voice I had ever heard. We hung out all day and by the evening I was smitten.

Tim was the opposite of me in terms of lifestyle: he worked in advertising and spent his days lunching with men in suits whilst I rolled around on studio floors and spent hours late into the night making music. He was a 9-5 man and I was forever on tour. But the businessman was a guy who expressed how much respect he had for his sisters and mother and how much he cared about the planet… I knew that he had a feminist heart and for me this was all that mattered.

After two months Tim moved in. It didn't feel reckless or silly, just right. He unpacked his stuff into my tiny loft room in Clapton and we split the paltry £350 rent. That summer was paradise. But when I got back from Edinburgh and winter began to come on, everything changed.

One day in a rush into town I grabbed Tim's backpack to use for some heavy books and found several packets of Citalopram, a strong form of antidepressants I recognized from a family member's use. I was so shocked. I remember sitting down on the edge of the bed and bursting into tears. I knew Tim was in a big meeting with a newspaper all day so I sent him a distraught email, asking him to call me. As I waited for him to come home, I remember feeling like my bones were somehow sticking out of my body, totally broken.

What transpired was not at all what I expected. I waited patiently on our bed trying my best to remain levelheaded. I will never forget his face as he came through the door; he looked so broken. I remember us hugging for a very long time, it was very emotional. We lay on the bed staring at each other and started right from the beginning of the story. I had imagined he had been on the tablets for a little while and he had not told me because he felt embarrassed.

But what unfurled was a horrendous and year long breakdown at the age of twenty-two and nearly a decade of lying, self medicating and denial with suicidal episodes. I felt so much sadness for Tim and an overwhelming feeling of wanting to rescue him from his heavy shame that felt so misplaced. I had seen members of my family heavy under the weight of mental illness; I knew full well that it was a disease, not something that reflected a weakness in someone's personality.

I was of course rattled by the seismic shift in our relationship but I knew I would never leave Tim. His honesty and vulnerability made me love him so much more. Our relationship went from romantic and idyllic to deep and profound.

What followed was a period of coming out. Tim told his work about his struggles with mental illness, he told his friends, his family. He was met with nothing but kindness and respect. It transpired that other men he knew had also been struggling silently with poor mental health too. I read a lot, tooling up, I wanted to know what we were in for as Tim made the decision to gradually reduce his dose of Citalopram. I waited patiently to see who the man I loved was underneath the haze of drugs.

The first few months were hopeful, he seemed happier. But he was also a lot more sensitive to the world around him and sometimes irritable that he felt powerless in it. That winter was a struggle but it wasn't until about seven months later that the world caved in.

I was on tour in Australia during Spring 2014. Tim had been feeling increasingly unwell; fatigued, terrible headaches and an awful insomnia, all of which we now know are early onset signs of his depression. We put it down to a combination of winter blues and chemical readjustments. Three weeks in Tim had a massive breakdown, he was wandering around central London in a daze until he eventually made it home. I managed to Skype him at his parents' house and he looked like a shell of a man. He cried and said he had been thinking about death a lot and staring at our bedroom window imagining his body hanging from it. It was devastating. He went to the doctor and got a very high dose of tablets; I know he felt like a failure but we needed a quick fix to save him and it thankfully worked. Three weeks later he was feeling a bit more like himself.

When I returned I felt like I never wanted to be away again. I told him I wanted to give up touring or he would have to make a show with me. He said 'I know about two things in this world, advertising and mental illness'. I told him a show about advertising would be the worst, but a show about why men hide their depression would be infinitely excellent. He agreed he could use a break and that he would love to tour with me.

Making the show was a revelation for both of us. It was difficult to organize – in order for Tim to leave his salary meant I had to have gigs and development funds sorted before we had even set foot in the studio. I was used to working with non-artists, having made a show with my nine-year-old niece but this was much harder. It was a sensitive subject and Tim has NEVER been onstage. He was wooden, nervy and gangly. But it quickly transpired that this was the joy of the project; that he was just an ordinary guy trying his best to muddle through. He learnt to dance, to play the guitar. It was magical.

I never wanted to put words into his mouth, so the show revolved around a series of candid interviews we made in our living room, where he felt most confortable being honest. He laid down some rules. The most important one was that he never wanted to have to look the audience in the eye; so we created a series of elaborate head coverings that represented different periods of his story. He exists behind these masks for nearly all of the show, until the finale. It was such a beautiful rule because it so accurately summarized his history.

We have toured our show across Australia thus far and the response has been overwhelming. It's a modern love story, our lives laid bare, brutally honest. Our main aim was to make it as entertaining and funny as possible. We have had so many emails from people connecting with us and sharing stories.

I am five months pregnant now and spending our days together is heavenly. We are currently prepping to tour the UK for a few months and will again in Spring after the baby is born. Tim is on a low dose of tablets at the moment and doing really well. We know our lives will be always filled with mental illness. We talk every day and have both resolved to always be activists in the sphere of mental health awareness. Tim to me represents true love incarnate – something way deeper than I could have ever imagined when I went out to drink gin that night.

TIM'S STORY

When Bryony found those little tablets in my bag two years ago it felt like I had been found out. I didn't want her to know I needed a tablet to stop me from constantly crying. All she needed to know was that I was the happy, fun and reckless laugh I thought she fancied. It certainly beat the scared, tired, teary, confused, suicidal, hopeless, angry me. Now there was no going back. She wanted to know everything.

I was twenty-two when I woke up one morning and tears just fell and I didn't know why. I began a spiral into sadness. I couldn't sleep, I just kept crying, I felt physically deflated and didn't feel myself at all. After six months I had my first suicidal thought. Code red, time to go to the family GP. After a few weeks of taking Citalopram, an anti-depressant medication, the

UNIVERSITY OF WINCHESTER LIBRARY

old me came back, I stopped crying and I enjoyed things I used to enjoy. Then began eight years of secretly taking the tablets without anyone knowing other than my parents…

That night, Bryony was like a curious medical student analyzing every word of my confession. To my surprise this secret of mine made her love me even more. My openness, the complexity of my emotions and the vulnerability of my well-being – she told me that being a man to her was all this, as well as being able to knock up a couple of shelves.

This was the start of coming to terms with my illness. I had used the old food poisoning excuse at work too many times when I had attempted to come off the tablets or the depression had intensified. I was ready to find out exactly what was wrong with my brain and face up to it.

Telling all to Bryony was the first step; not too bad. Telling my mates was next, this worried me because I thought I would be excluded from the 'lads' part of a group of male mates. Nothing changed – if anything it gave us a license to talk about our problems. I don't know how we thought for so long that none of us had any issues. Another stupid blokey thing. It transpires that a couple of us had mental health problems.

I'd made the decision to come off my anti-depressants a couple of times. I was twenty-six the first time I tried. I was doing well at work and having the time of my life in London. I thought I don't need these tablets anymore. I couldn't be happier. Naively, I just came off them cold turkey and after three weeks it came crashing back on top of me. Straight back on the tablets. The second time was four years later. With Bryony by my side we planned it meticulously, by the book. I changed my diet, stopped drinking and doing all the things that could interfere with my recovery. I weened myself off the medication over a three-month period on the advice of the doctors. I felt great. I was back. Then another three months later the depression crept back. The experiment had failed, again. I was pretending it was working for too long and let it develop until I couldn't take any more. Bryony was in Australia on tour which didn't help, I didn't have my home doctor who had been by my side all the

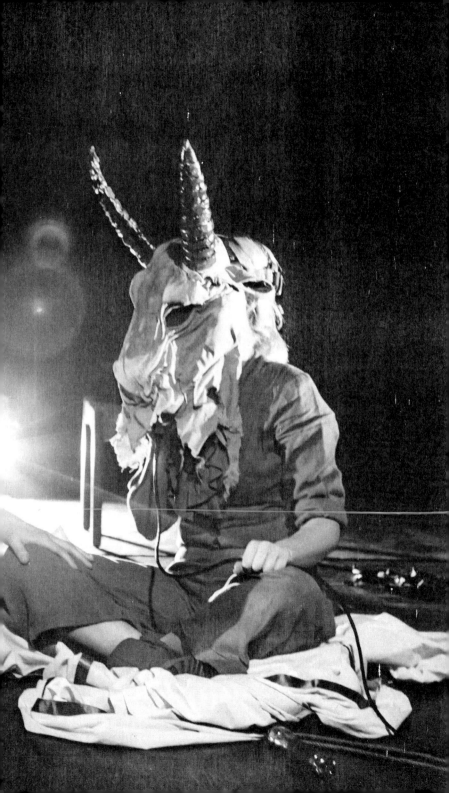

way through. It hit me hard and I had a breakdown. Within a few days I was back on the tablets.

It was around this time that I realized that I just wasn't up to my job and I needed time to figure this all out. I told my boss. Result: supportive, understanding and probably a relief of not being lied to with another dodgy chicken dinner story. Still, I was a bit scared. I had worked in advertising for the past eight years, things were going well and I was due a promotion. However, I thought this was an opportunity that doesn't come too often, so the job could wait.

All of these reactions led Bryony and I to discuss the idea of telling all who wanted to listen about the damage caused by concealing a mental illness – a problem that male sufferers are particulary prone to. I'd had the hardest discussions, with family, girlfriend, friends and colleagues already, so it didn't really matter who else knew.

The idea of making a theatre show was exciting and terrifying. I was a nervous wreck even putting on a PowerPoint presentation to a few colleagues and now I had to get my head around talking about crying in cubicles to 250 strangers every night. It took a while to realize that this is what I had agreed to do, but because I had that encouragement from Bryony, I trusted her to make something good. We wanted it to be completely honest with no theatrical thrills. Depression could have killed me and it has killed millions of people so we had to be sensitive. It had to be raw or I wouldn't have felt like I could do it. It felt like a big job.

I looked back to when I was twenty-one and wasn't depressed – I had to admit that I probably didn't believe the illness existed myself. I thought it was just for people who couldn't hack it. A member of my family suffered for years, but as kids were weren't to know that. What a load of old rubbish. To research the show, I read everything I could get my hands on; I went to seminars with people from the UN and loads of doctors who knew about the brain.

Then, suddenly, we were at the Edinburgh Fringe 2014 with our work in progress. It was August 2014, the first time I've ever been on stage. I froze, I forgot everything I was supposed to say. Thankfully I had my professional girlfriend next to me who carried the show. People loved it. We had passed the test and it was time to really give it a go. We took *Fake It 'Til You Make It* to Australia, and by show twenty-five, I had started to enjoy it a little, though I couldn't stop shaking. The postive feedback is one of the best feelings I've ever had. I will never forget an email I got from a young lad who saw the show and he said that he's been battling these dark thoughts everyday for a year, he was suicidal. He said that seeing the show made him do something about it and see a doctor.

I've made more progress in this incredible year with regards to my mental health than I had in the eight years keeping it a secret. I'm not bowling around pretending I've got nothing wrong with me. This is who I am, this has been a part of my life and now I like to think I'm getting better. I'm on a very low dose of medication now and I reckon in four months I may not need it any more.

I haven't made my mind up about what I'm going to do when this is all over. I've always wanted to try screen acting but never had the confidence. But I also did enjoy my job and loved the people in it. I'll just have to see what happens. One thing I have realized is that you've got to be a machine to be perfect, imperfections are part of what makes us who we are.

This is the script from August 2015, from the Traverse as part of the Edinburgh Festival Fringe. At this time Bryony is seven months pregnant.

BRYONY: Bryony Kimmings

TIM: Tim Grayburn

Director Bryony Kimmings

Dramaturg Nina Steiger

Sound Design and Music Tom Parkinson and Matt Lewis

Lighting Designer Nao Nagai

Art Direction David Curtis Ring

Costume David Curtis Ring and Olivia Deur

Props David Curtis Ring

Set Design Amelia Jane Hankin

Production Manager Beth O'Leary

General Manager Jo Salkilld

Administrator Amy Davies Dolamore

Commissioned by Southbank Centre (London) Theatre Works (Melbourne) with Soho Theatre. Supported by DanceXchange, Arts Council England, Peggy Ramsay Foundation and donations made by the brilliant people on Kickstarter, namely…

Roz Wyllie, Ruth Holdsworth, Helen Ody, Francesca Seeley, Sarah Longfield, Jodie Gibson, Rachael Marshall, Helen Draper, Nika Obydzinski, Sal Culmer, Paul Bogen, Stuart Douglas, Jordana Golbourn, Gina Krone, Rachele Bowley, Jess Brandler, Laura Muldoon, Mark Burborough, Ellie Sikorski, Ruby Carr, Thomas W, Susannah Day, Sam Bennett, David Cahill Roots, Tomos James, Naomi Steward, Jack Gouldbourne, Bridget Symonds, Tracy harris, Clare Reddington, Cassandra Miller, KILN (formerly Kindle Theatre), Ewelina Kolaczek, Gaynor Williams, Jess Flanagan, Elouise Farley, Emma Kerr, Amy Smith, Lee Smith, Nathan Allison, Robert Stanton, Fiona Ryan, Danny Weddup, Lesley Quilty, Anthony Newton, Joanna Griffin, Amy Letman, Jonathan Wakeham, Keren Nicol, Tatton Spiller, Julia Haworth, Amy Saunders, Phoebe Elliott, Rebecca Quinn, Lisa, Maddie Hennessy, Sarah Blanc, Anne Lawson, Gilly Matthews, Ellie Julier, Diana Ware, Adrienne Truscott, Kay Jamieson, Mary Halton, Scott Field, Jo Young, Frehd, Christopher May, Drew Taylor, Jordan McKenzie, Caroline Campbell, Andy Mellor, Cookie Arnone, Paul Mellor, Chris Sonnex, Philippa Barr, Katherine Hollinson, Anita Wadsworth, Philip, Danielle Rose, Jakub Krupa, Mel Scaffold, Camilla Whitehill, Sarah Plasted, Jenny, Clair Korobacz, Cheryl Collins, Mary Jane Hetzlein, Axel, Millie Whelan, Marc McKay, Emily Rich, John Boursnell, Jake Orr, Anais Higgins, Annah Lång, Róise Goan, Lara Hickey, Helena Sherriff, Benjamin Corry Wright Kootbaully, Max Humphries, Valentina Ceschi, Simon Martin, Louise Taylor, MuddyMouth, Joe Robinson, Elouise Farley.

Act One

The stage is empty as the audience arrives. There is one open white back light on the stage, nothing flashy. The music is kind of industrial, repetitive and has a sense of impending doom. There are ropes in the rig strung across the rig in a diamond shape and coming down to fixed spots on the sides. The rope is orange. Just caught in the light.

The house lights and music fade.

BRYONY and TIM enter the auditorium. They have baskets on their heads and maraccas in their hands. They are in their underpants, very unflattering, spanx, y-fronts, maternity bra, crap white socks, BRYONY all in nude, TIM in white.

Tacky rhumba muzak begins to play and the duo sing a song doing a stupid and ugly dance routine on the spot which includes butt shaking and kicks.

1 – THE DOCTORS' SONG

B: 70% of patients sitting in the doctors' waiting room queue

Are there with mental health complaints

Now doesn't that just slightly shift the view

T: *(Whispered.)* That's seventy percent of you!

B: Don't make me go to the doctor

T: A broken arm ain't like a broken brain

B: Don't make me go to the doctor

T: He'll make me fill in that form again

B: Don't make me go the doctor

T: A broken arm ain't like a broken brain

B: Don't make me go to the doctor

T: Oh no not that form again

B: It can be up to 8% of us (that's 8% of us.) at any one time.

It will be 1 in 4 of us. That's a quarter love, some point in our busy lives.

T: *(Whispered.)* A mental health surprise.

B: Don't make me go to the doctor

T: A broken arm ain't like a broken brain

B: Don't make me go to the doctor

T: He'll make me fill in that form again

Dance break.

B: Don't make me go the doctor

T: A broken arm ain't like a broken brain

B: Don't make me go to the doctor

T: Oh no not that form again!

They bow, the lights fade.

In the blackout BRYONY walks to her microphone SR. TIM heads backstage to set himself for the movies scene with his binoculars and bag.

2 – PROLOGUE

She nods a hello to everyone. Very friendly and chatty delivery.

B: Hello.

I'm Bryony Kimmings. I'm a loud mouth…slightly heavily pregnant now, feminist performance artist from London. If you aren't familiar with my art work you can usually find me sniffing around some kind of social stigma or trying to tear down a terrible taboo. And I often work with people who don't usually grace the stage.

So, that was Tim Grayburn. He works in advertising. He is an account director at a big media agency back in London so his days are usually spent buying advertising space for big corporate brands…like Barclaycard. *(She boos.)*

Or I should say he used to, up until about six months ago when he decided to leave his job, make this show with me and come on tour for a year.

Now. If you didn't know it already Tim and I are a real life human being couple. So this unfortunately guys is going to be a love story. Sorry gross. But an unconventional one. One between two people that absolutely love the film *Dumb and Dumber*, or two people who like to make fart noises when the other one bends down in public spaces, but a love story nonetheless.

And as with all love stories, in the movies, in books… or on the stage, we had to leave quite a lot of stuff out. Because they only give you an hour. So we decide to remove, for your viewing pleasure, the mundanity of everyday existence.

31

…ike, in the first draft we took out the scene 'Why Am I Making Breakfast When I Fucking Made It Yesterday?!". We recently made the dramaturgical decision to remove the morning sickness dance routine, and just before we came on we cut a whole song called 'My Black Sock Or Yours – The Laundry Day Debacle'.

But what we couldn't remove was all the darkness, all the god forsaken bleak stuff. Because this is a show about clinical depression, more specifically clinical depression and men and the women that love those men. And this is a true story, based around just two and a half years of life together and it centres around a series of recordings made by Tim and I in our lounge back in London.

We have tried our best to balance out the darkness with as much light and pizazz as we possibly can!

Pause.

Look… I am a very superstitious person. Especially when it comes to being onstage. So I have made something to look after us while we share this space together. This is a Japanese luck doll. He will watch over us, bring us luck. I will hang him here for the duration of the show.

(She pauses, pulls a serious face.) Good luck everyone!

(Moves away from her mic shouting loud.) Now on with the love story people!

3 – JUST LIKE THE MOVIES

Epic side light and smoke fill the space as the pair walk towards each other in slow motion like in a movie. TIM now has a backpack on and a pair of binoculars firmly held to his face. Ennio Morricone music plays…filmic and loud. They somehow manage to miss one another when they finally get to the bit where they should embrace. It's funny.

The music abruptly cuts.

4 – THIS IS TIM

B: This is Tim Grayburn, up close and personal in his pants.

He is a man, a real man.

The strong silent type.

TIM is nervous, he shifts his weight.

He is thirty-two years old. He is a Gemini if you go in for all of that and he is my fiancé.

He has dark brown curly hair that he absolutely hates and his body is covered in approximately 1 million freckles. I once promised Tim I would lay him in a gallery and count all of those freckles as some kind of meta love/art project, so that will probably be our next work together Tim. *(He bristles nervously.)*

I asked Tim his top three favourite things to do so you could get to know him a bit better. He said he loved playing football, eating dinner out and having sex. Classics!

But I can add, so you can get to know him a little better, that he is kind and very laid back. He has a terrible memory, has always wished he could play the guitar ever since he was a child but never learnt, and he takes great pleasure in hiding and then making people jump, which I absolutely hate.

Tim agreed to make this show with me just after Robin Williams died. But because the job was so far removed from his everyday life he gave me some fundamental rules that I had to follow.

Rule number ONE. He didn't want to have to look any of you lot in the eye. *(TIM reveals that his binoculars are indeed stuck to his face as he puts his arms down.)*

Rule number TWO. He didn't feel like he had any tangible stage skills so he asked *(She holds the mic for his mouth and he speaks nervously and like an ordinary human.)*

T: If I could learn how to play the guitar.

B: So we got him some lessons and he is doing alright. *(She shakes her head and betrays him, that he is in fact terrible.)* And THREE. He wanted to always appear like a real man. I thought of Robert Redford in *Out of Africa.*

(Gestures to his pants. They laugh.) Done, I think you'll agree!

TIM heads towards the plinth in front of him and kneels. He takes off his backpack and takes out a small brass machine covered by a glass box and places it on the plinth as BRYONY speaks. It lights up.

Now let's start at the beginning of the story. Long before I was seven months pregnant with our son, before we got our embarrassing matching tattoos. *(She lifts her arm.)* For a very long time, almost eight years, Tim kept his mental illness a secret from everyone he knew… including me.

The lights fade. Apart for the one on the machine.

TIM goes backstage, BRYONY heads into the audience.

5 – RECORDING 1

The machine turns on, begins to spin under the glass. We hear BRYONY and TIM talking in their lounge.

Laughter.

B: **Um can you tell me or us a little bit about your childhood?**

T: Alright, um, I grew up in quite a big family, grew up in a nice little village, um, beautiful little village, no stress. Just a pub, a school, a shop and that was it. Uh, quite a conventional family really, Mum and Dad together, happy, Dad went to work every day, a strong sort of typical man. Yeah at the weekends he would build houses, he would build our house that we lived in, so he would always be doing something physical yeah.

B: Depression? Was that ever mentioned?

T: No, never, didn't have a clue what it meant.

The machine turns off, its lights fade.

6 – TRUE LOVE

BRYONY is in the audience confiding in someone.

B: I guess you could say I was looking for true love. Someone to knock my socks off, or sweep me off my feet, or who just got me. I think secretly Tim was too BUT I think we might have also resigned ourselves to the fact we were maybe never going to meet that special someone. So when Tim and I finally did meet we fell in love hard and we fell fast! And what started as a one-night stand in a dirty East London nightclub became the seminal and historic moment where we both meet the love of our lives. And we rolled in fields of one endless, reckless summer and it was paradise… He was like this beast running amok in Hackney. But I didn't want to tame him, just chase him and soak him up. God it sounds so clichéd. I can even remember saying to mother on the telephone at the time, as gross as this sounds that it was like someone had sent him to me from heaven.

7 – OLD FASHIONED WALK

'Old Fashioned Walk' by Perry Como suddenly begins to play. TIM comes onstage and BRYONY runs towards him from the audience. TIM has clouds on his head, the lights are soft focus, yellows and pinks. They duo dance like they are courting and in love. Like Ginger Rogers and Fred Astaire. Then at the end of the dance the duo snog and grope each other fiercely. They chase one another offstage frantically tearing at each others' clothes.

8 – RECORDING 2

The machine turns on, its light comes up.

T: **I was around twenty-three/twenty-four, can't exactly remember when but something changed completely in me, I was really tired all the time, I just woke up different. Um, I didn't want to hang around with my mates anymore, I didn't want to do things I loved doing like playing football and seeing friends. Um, I just thought I'm tired and that's basically it, I just need to deal with it myself. I wouldn't have even dreamed of going to the doctors.**

The machine turns off, as does its light.

9 – BUILDING A HOME

B: *(Walking on stage.)* Three months into the love story and the bugger moved in!

Music begins, Ennio Morricone again, epic and grand. Warm lights again, pinks and yellows fade up. TIM drags his belonging in a pile across the stage. The duo smile at the audience and each other. A little home making scene begins. They unpack. The pair build themselves a tent in unison and like a dance. The tent is light green with bronze buckles. Really neat and new.

BRYONY comes out of the tent and puts little good luck dolls along the guy ropes and smiles at the audience, knowing she is being superstitious and silly. TIM checks all the ropes. He still has the clouds on his head. Puts out some plants.

The only thing that hasn't been brought into the tent is the machine and BRYONY notices it for the first time. At the end of the scene BRYONY picks it up and tries to bring it inside but TIM hurridly stops her, she is confused and wants to bring it inside, instead he hurries her into the house, she looks back at it wondering what it is. He places it back on its plinth and tries to cover her eyes and she goes inside confused.

10 – RECORDING 3

The machine turns on. The lights fade down to just the machine and a little glow on the tent where BRYONY and TIM hang out their blue linen costumes as washing and then change slowly into them as the recording plays. TIM wears light blue linen trousers and matching top, pulling matching braces over his shoulders and boots of identical colour onto his feet. BRYONY wears dark blue linen functional trousers and a matching shirt with a ruffle neck, done up tight, her boots match too. The costume is cartoon like because everything matches in colour completely but also very American gothic in its references, very gendered.

T: *I didn't realize how, how dark, how dark it would get and how it would effect everyone around me. Erm. I… I woke up one morning and tears just poured out of my face into my pillow. Erm I just. I couldn't believe what was going on to be honest, I hadn't cried for years and all of sudden I am waking up nothing bad had happened in the family, nothing bad really in particular in my life and I'm crying my eyes out at nine o'clock in the morning.*

And it just got worse and worse as the days went on.
I just could not sleep at night, I was just up thinking
about random stuff like 'Why are we all here? what's the
point of it? we all die in the end anyway so what's the
point of all these relationships you keep and the people
you love are just going to disappear one day.' I felt like
I wanted to talk about it, but I just couldn't I was too
ashamed. My dad, my dad, wouldn't have had a clue he
would have just said I just need to get on with it.

There was a tree when I was a kid that I used to play at
and I used to stop there for like twenty mins or so just
staring at it and images of myself were just popping into
my head of me hanging there. I wasn't really shocked
and I wasn't scared I was just, get upset and I would cry
because I have those thoughts. I would go home and think
about where I'd get the rope from, how I'd do it. Erm I
just thought, it just popped into my head and I guess, I
guess it was something telling me that this is a way out if
you want it. Until, I was so tired, so upset, so sad, I didn't
know what was going on, I basically had a breakdown
in front of the family one evening at the dinner table.
And ah, erm and then, and then, my mum said enough is
enough and she took me to the doctors and I just sat there
with a head full of muddled thoughts asking them to try
and make me better.

The duo have made their way to their stools outside the tent and
sat down.

The machine turns off.

Pause.

11 – GENDER DANCE

Planningtorock's sound 'Let's talk about gender baby' plays loudly. The lights snap to bright colourful pools of yellow and pink.

The duo are in sunglasses seated on stools outside the tent. TIM has a hammer down his trousers and BRYONY has a whisk.

The pair do a dance routine together. Pretending to be boys and girls and everything in-between. They prance, they party, they produce a hammer and whisk from their pants. It's funny and weird.

Until they find themselves downstage centre and next to one another. The music warps and changes. Slightly more sinister now. They speak in unison in monotonous almost robot-like voices into their mics. Kind of Kraftwerk-like.

B&T: Quick it's a boy

Quick give that boy a truck

Quick get your boob out and give that boy a suck

(They begin to march in unison on the spot.)

Quick make him tough now

Don't ever let him cry

Show him only heterosexual love

But don't tell him why

(They begin to move backwards to the mouth of the tent.)

Quick give him limits

Don't let him show his feelings

Tell him a lady's only job is staring at the ceiling

39

Quick show him power is only found in strength

Don't let him know that talking

Can help him see some sense

(They stop marching.)

And if he's feeling sad now

Don't let him tell you so

Just say that hiding sport and beer

Is the only way to go

(TIM goes slowly to collect his cloud head, taking his shades off and putting it back on his head like he's getting ready for work.)

B: *(On her own now.)*

Quick let him go to work now

Every single day

Even if he feels his brain is about to waste away

The music ends. BRYONY sets her mic and whisk down. Takes off her sunglasses and smoothes her clothes down. She kisses TIM on the cheek and he slowly heads to work. Walking like a slow stone giant statue to his microphone. A rumble sound begins. BRYONY waves him off like a good housewife, when he is out of sight she glares at the machine and heads inside.

12 – TIM AT WORK

TIM's mic spot snaps up and the mood changes. We are at TIM's work.

T: Good morning all,

On the agenda for this week's meeting is:

A look at the weekly monitor, who are the winners and losers of the market.

Rates – what we can do to improve our ROI. And lastly, more importantly, tools to grow revenue and ultimately improve our bottom line.

BRYONY peaks out of the tent. Creeps out. She hangs out more good luck dolls and sits shadily on her chair staring at the machine which lights up.

The market as a whole is down 26.8% week on week. There are a number of factors for this, the week previous was one of the biggest spending weeks for advertisers this year. It's likely cash will now be saved in the upcoming weeks. We must capitalise on this and stretch the market while it's fluid.

BRYONY walks sheepishly towards the machine, the machine makes a sound like it is trying to turn on. She looks up in the air. He hears it somehow too and looks up into the air. He stumbles over his words.

Erm…ahhh… As you all know, we have the most discounted rates in the industry due to the buying power of the group. I need you all to push each negotiation as far as it goes in the next coming weeks, squeeze out of them what you can.

She touches the box with her finger, it tries to start up again. Again he can hear it calling him, it throws him.

Erm…er… The money we save here will go into supporting new clients, new clients that pay us well and keep the FD's and board members happy.

She picks it up and shakes it, once more it gurgles and starts. He falters. She makes her way backwards across the stage.

Guys… Get on your planning systems, figure out how we're going to reach our target audiences in the most cost effective way.

Danny, if you don't mind I want you come to next week's meeting with a deck on results…

The machine turns on and he stops dead, they both hear his voice, her at home, him at work.

T: ***I would have to take myself to work in an absolute wreck and try and put on a fake smile in front of everyone and hold back the tears.***

There is a massive sound of an explosion and the lights flare brightly. TIM is literally blasted away from his office presentation and onto the floor BRYONY flies across the stage. Blackout.

13 – BRY'S EMAIL

A cold light comes onto BRYONY, who is holding the machine.

B: Oh gosh Tim.

I have got myself into a right tizz. I know it's a busy day for you so ignore my text. I thought it better to send an email anyway.

I grabbed your black backpack to pop my laptop in to take into town.

I emptied it as it looked just like gym stuff, I thought you wouldn't mind, but in it I found some Citalopram. Now I know what these are as my mum used to take them and Han had them for her bi-polar for two years and they were awful emotion blockers.

I didn't know you took them?! Did I?

I am wracking my brains to figure out if this is something HUGE that I did know…

But I am not finding the information anywhere. I was very shocked when I found them. I had to sit down on the edge of the bed.

I want to talk to you about it. Can you call me. I am wondering why I didn't know, seeing as we are so close to one another. Or I think we are. I am sorry if that seems awfully dramatic, but I can't put these two pieces of information together: my lovely, open, happy Tim and these drugs that I have seen turn my nearest into zombies.

Am I being a twat?!

Love you, Bry

With that there is another explosion and flash and BRYONY *is blasted away from her microphone too.*

Pause.

14 – DARK THOUGHTS

BRYONY'*s face is lit by a tiny light in the machine. She wanders in shock towards* TIM. *He is stumbling about to get out. They peer into it, heading to the plinth. They are whispering and speaking slowly.*

T: What is that?

B: It's another way of not talking about it I guess.

T: No…it's not

B: It's some kind of incubator lighting up our faces?

They place the box on its plinth. It lights up brightly, lighting their faces.

T: No it's not. It's a machine, functioning but with its wires all mixed up

B: It looks like it is hard at work, digging away underneath all that glass.

Pause. She looks up at the light on the machine.

I think it's some kind of metaphor?

T: Don't be wanky

B: Whatever it is, I think we should leave it to do its job

T: OK but I think we need to look after it.

They walk away into the darkness.

Act Two

15 – DESTINY

BRYONY is on the doorstep of the tent.

B: The day I found Tim's tablets; was the day that the love story changed. I remember he came home from work that evening very much expecting his bags to be packed and on the front doorstep. But instead we sat up late into the night and talked everything through, it was hard going. For Tim is was the first time that he had said these things aloud to another living soul.

He said that he was relieved that the secret was finally out. That he had actually felt better for a really long time. That what he was having trouble with was not the depression but rather the side effects from the tablets he was taking. He said he really want to come off them.

BRYONY sets up a microphone stand and moves the stools out of the way.

He told me he had tried to go cold turkey in the past but it hadn't worked out well.

Pause.

Me. I felt confused. Deceived and more than a little bit worried. I wondered where my true love had gone, who was this man living in my house. But when I looked into his eyes late that night I saw the shattered remains of my beast staring right back at me, so I agreed to help him.

TIM comes onstage and joins BRYONY with his guitar, this time he is wearing blackout glasses, they make him look like someone in a magazine who doesn't want their identity known.

B: The next day I went to my studio, buoyed up with hope and ambition for our future together. And I wrote Tim a really embarrassing love song that we are quite mortified to have to perform now…

Tim's on guitar.

This is Destiny.

Music begins, BRYONY nudges TIM and TIM pretends to play the guitar and they do a dance routine as they sing.

B: Some people go for the opposite

Some people go for the eyes

Some people fail just for the fun of it

Those people aren't like you and I

Some creatures never seem miss a trick

Some creatures never get it right

Some creatures forever run away from it

Those creatures aren't like you and I

Because what we have is different

We work hard until it works

We can never be complacent

We can't ignore it if it hurts

And I'll tell you till the cows come home

And I'll tell you till I'm horse

The future is mapped out for us

I promise this of course…

I'll hold your hand

And I'll dry your eyes

And I'll never you

Never deceive you

Your destiny is mine

And I'll break your fucking legs

If you ever leave

I'll always keep you

Never mistreat you…

Your destiny, your destiny, is me

TIM misses the final guitar strum and it's funny. He bumbles off to his mic. BRYONY moves her mic stand.

16 – THAT TIME

Each at their mics.

B: The next part of the story looked like this…

T: We stopped drinking

B: We read all the books

T: I started to look after myself better

B: I spoke to my mum on the phone a lot

T: I told all my mates

B: I didn't tell my friends

T: Turns out some of them had it too

B: Because I loved him

T: I loved her

B: We found ourselves a new GP

T: I laughed at myself

B: I secretly had the idea for this show

T: I told work and secretly wanted to leave

B: Autumn became winter

Winter became spring

And the drugs they dwindled down

And our little house became a library full of scheming and research

And for a while we took great comfort from the things we learnt about Tim's brain.

17 – SSRI'S

TIM is putting his guitar away and setting a little table with objects in the black. He stands next to a little table at the mouth of the tent with a tablet in his hand. On the table is the hammer, the whisk, a string of chillies, a good luck doll, a ball of wet tissue and a strap to fit TIM's head.

BRYONY is pretending to be a nurse doing a demonstration about Anti-Depressants. She speaks in a cockney presentation voice. She uses TIM as a mannequin. Building him up like a weather map of tablet side effects. Moving him around the stage. The lights are clinical.

B: SSRI's or selective serotonin reuptake inhibitors are a type of anti-depressant tablet for people with clinical depression.

She marches over to TIM. He is getting things sorted on stage.

Serotonin is a neurotransmitter in the brain associated with happiness and wellbeing.

The depressed brain reuptakes Serotonin too quickly, thus resulting in low mood.

She swirls her hand around the top of TIM's head. He spins.

These tablets balance out that re-uptake…thus making you happier.

Now they are very effective, used by millions across the world BUT they also have some pretty major side effects. Side effects Tim had been labouring under for quite some time.

For example, they can blur your vision.

She points to his blackout glasses.

They can make your body temperature go up by a few degrees thus producing excessive and embarrassing sweating.

She places the string of chillies round his neck and mimes sweat spraying out of his armpits onto the audience.

They can give you headaches, Tim suffered with migraines for many years. They can give you insomnia, *(She straps the hammer to his head.)* brain zaps, little electric shocks around the temples that can be pretty painful, and in some rare cases they can give you suicidal thoughts…

She is herself again for a moment…

But depression gives you suicidal thoughts, so…

Back to cockney nurse…

Swings and roundabouts I guess?!

Pause.

They can give you indigestion, especially if you take them before you eat your breakfast and they can also make you pretty queasy if they are strong. *(He whizzes the whisk in his tummy when instructed.)*

They can numb your feelings *(She punches him on the arm.)* give you a really dry mouth.

She sticks the ball of tissue in his mouth.

And they can also make your libido go down. (Not that we ever had any problems like that!) *(She pops a little good luck doll down his pants.)*

It takes about three months to come off them effectively. You reduce your dose slowly week-by-week monitored by your doctor assessing whether the side effects are going away, or if the symptoms of depression are creeping back in. So on the advice of our GP, that's what we did.

He spits the tissue out of his mouth and lowers his head. He removes the whisk and the hammer and slowly walks to the tent, going inside and hiding. BRYONY looks sadly after him and then back to the audience.

B: *(In a low measured voice.)* Turns out men don't talk about their mental health that much.

Turns out that much more of a 'typically female trait'.

Turns out they don't present emotional symptoms to the doctor.

She moves the little table aside.

That they are much more likely to present with physical pains or with addictions related to their depression. Turns out the problem wasn't the tablets.

Excuse me.

She goes into the tent and closes the door.

18 – RECORDING 5

The machine turns on, lights up. The tent is bathed in a low blue.

T: **The doctors gave me like a really good plan, and they told me to wean myself off very gradually over a period of about three months. The usual stuff like look after yourself, don't drink too much, do a lot of exercise, eat well. There was quite a lot of hope from the doctor there wasn't actually any point where she said, don't get your hopes up too much as you might have to come straight back on them. I'd been on them for so many years because I hadn't thought about what exactly it was, I was just taking the tablets to get rid of what the doctor told me I had. I think I was waiting to feel settled and uh, have someone to do it with, yeah. In my heart of hearts I thought, if we did everything right, did it by the book, came off them gradually I would never have to take them again in my life. It was about two weeks, three weeks after I took my last tablet...and I started**

to notice that, that happy mood that I was in that I'd finished taking the medication was slowly disappearing and I started to not sleep as well again, um but I was still really hopeful that it was just a little bad stint and it would go away but it didn't.

The machine and its light turn off.

19 – PAPERBAG HEAD

Lovely pink and yellow lights come up, reminding us of better times.

The Carpenters 'Close to You' begins to play.

BRYONY opens the door of the tent. She steps out of their house looking up at the sky smiling. Then TIM emerges. He has a paper bag over his head. He is not responsive to anything. His body is stiff. Empty.

She walks forward with him and looks up at him adoringly.

She tries to play badminton with the good luck dolls but he doesn't hit back.

She walks along chatting away to him. No response. In fact he stops and stares out into the audience and she has to walk back and remind him.

She points out the view and he doesn't turn his head.

She tries to slow dance with him but he doesn't respond. His arms just fall down to his sides.

She kisses the mouth of the paperbag head and he moves back, her weight pushing him away. She wipes her mouth, confused.

She hurries to his side and takes his hand like she is encouraging him to remember. She performs the dance they did in an earlier scene to Perry Como but he just trails along when pulled and pushed.

She rolls into his arms and he drops her… She screams silently with her back to him, rushes to the box and holds it over her head as if she is about to smash it. Then she changes her mind and calmly puts it down smoothing her clothes down. The pair back away from each other and sit down on their stools, much further apart than before.

The Carpenters tune begins to warp into a slow repetitive drone, with drums building underneath. BRYONY brings her mic to her mouth in a slow stylistic movement. Reading out texts.

B: Hi Darling,

Just checking in.

You seemed a little blue this weekend at Granny's and I just wanted to say maybe come home straight from work tonight and we can sit down on the sofa and chat it all through? Maybe we need to go back to the doctors.
Bry

Pause.

Hi darling just wanted to check you are coming home straight after work…text me back xx

Pause.

Tim i've tried you a couple of times can you call me back

Pause.

Tim have you left work. I'm worried

The drums are building now and TIM is frantically ripping at the bag on his head, tearing it to pieces.

Tim?

Are you there?

He begins to rip his own paper bag off his head and she begins to freak out with her hands all over her hair and face. They both finish with the music, pause and run away.

20 – RECORDING 6

TIM walks back onstage, he is wearing the head of a great beast with horns. He staggers. He stalks the stage and heads to the machine and lowers himself around it as if to protect it.

The machine turns on.

T: I left, I left work one day and I remember it was a relief coming out of the office, but then as soon as I was out of the office I was even more scared about how I was feeling, I didn't know how I was going to get home. I got on a bus. Realised immediately that it was the wrong bus. Erm, I started to stress out as people were looking at me,

I got a fag out, started smoking it, someone even said 'put it out what are you doing' so I had to get off the bus. The confusion in my head was just something I've never had before. I went to cross the road and almost got hit by a car, people were shouting at me telling me to get off the road, get out of the way. And, I must have looked awful, I must have looked like a man who didn't know what he was going, where he was going, a man who'd lost his mind. And at that point I realised I was going to have to call you because I wasn't going to be able to get home otherwise.

BRYONY appears at the back of the stage, she appears to be driving.

21 – I AM DRIVING INTO CENTRAL LONDON

BRYONY drives across the stage. The drone is back and loud and full of doom.

B: So I'm driving into Central London and it's raining. And the windscreen wipers on the car are broken so they are making the sound of howling dogs on the windscreen. And I am trying not to panic and I am trying not to speed, but you haven't sounded like yourself on the phone so I'm doing both of those things.

TIM moves backwards from the plinth to the tent with his machine, protecting it, long sweeping animal-like strides. He watches her.

And you haven't been able to be very specific about where you are. Because you weren't making much sense. So I am making a bet that because of the time of day it is you are probably somewhere near your work. So I decide to park up and start walking my way around the grid system, looking out for you…or your bag…or your coat.

And I'm panicking because I've never seen you in full breakdown mode before and I am worried that I might fuck it up. Like should I take you to the hospital or just to the doctors? Like should I take you back to your parents or just to our flat? What if you're out of control, what if I can't physically get you into the car.

Drum music begins to build over the drone.

That beast…my beast, so wild and free but what if I don't recognise him and he doesn't recognise me.

Loud music begins. Very very loud. Drums, bass, noise. And both BRYONY and TIM fly into action.

22 – THE BEAST

TIM races around the stage in his beast head, banging it against the wall. Falling dangerously onto the floor over and over. Mimicking BRYONY at her mic. Skidding and falling and being out of control, shaking the tent. going loopy. Dancing like a maniac and holding onto his head in pain. Sometimes doing some of the love dance but getting it muddled and spinning around and dropping to the floor. He is very confused.

At the same time BRYONY is trying to organise the house and keep him safe. She can't work out where to put the machine. She is panicking. She packs up the furniture outside the tent, she shuts the door, she tries to get him in but for a long time he is out of control. She takes the box in and out of the tent, she throws tens of good luck dolls in the air around the perimeter of their plot.

TIM begins to bow at the audience again and again, like in the love dance. BRYONY comes out of the tent with the machine and puts her hand out to calm him, tame him.

And as the music reaches a deafening crescendo TIM does a gigantic bow and they finally collide centre stage. Knocking each other off balance and rocking around.

The music slows and TIM falls to his knees at BRYONY's feet. BRYONY is stroking his beasts head and TIM is breathing slow and hard. she has the machine in her arms. For a moment all seems lost.

She helps him up and the music changes. It is a slow and acoustic version of their Destiny song. They stumble back inside the tent all closed up tight. BRYONY puts the machine on the doormat and leaves it outside the tent.

23 – DESTINY SLOW

Once inside BRYONY turns on a torch and in the circle of the torchlight the pair are projected onto the tent canvas. BRYONY helps TIM take off his beast head. She wipes his brow and kisses his forehead. She puts her head down. He lifts her chin and kisses her.

The recording device turns on.

T: Like um, after I got ill again, just seeing how worried you were…made me sort of feel like a failure again I guess and er, felt like I was back at the start basically. Erm…dunoo I just thought that I was back to being useless and couldn't hack it and I wasn't tough enough to get through it without these tablets…and then er I thought that perhaps that's it then forever um, and I just thought it might be better if I left you too it.

They put their heads together for a moment.

They embrace.

He falls away from view and she is left alone.

She looks from her left to her right.

B: Tim?

The music ends.

Tim?

The tent falls slowly down over her.

UNIVERSITY OF WINCHESTER LIBRARY

Act Three

24 – SEARCH LIGHT

There is a pause and BRYONY suddenly flails under the sheet, panicking. She takes the torch and frees herself of the tent and stands up. Nothing can be seen apart from her torch light. TIM isn't there.

She shines the torch into her hand and we see her face light up, she is searching the room with her eyes. Looking for her true love.

She shines the torch onto the audience looking for him.

B: Tim?

She shines the torchlight on the floor as if searching for a body in long grass.

She shines the torch into the rig looking for a body.

She hears something behind her.

She spins round and slowly shines her torch up TIM's body on the opposite side of the stage. He is trying to escape. Caught in the act.

TIM has a tangled mass of rope over his whole head. A stark low light comes up on him. Frozen.

BRYONY goes to him, she tries to remove his rope head twice, both times he stops her. She gives up and turns him round from the audience to protect him.

The recording machine turns on. This time it is BRYONY's voice.

26 – RECORDING 8

B: **When I think of you being ill, at my most terrified…that makes me most terrified… Like our bedroom window, I couldn't look at it after you'd said about it. I couldn't**

**even open it. I imagined, ooh i'm gonna cry now, I…
haha.** *(Crying, voice trembling.)* **Like what would I do if I
found you there?** *(Voice breaks.)* **and you were still alive,
how would I get you down? How would I go get you? But
I kind of understand its not that you want to do that but
I didn't really, like what would I do, how would I rescue
you?** *(Sound of TIM kissing BRYONY.)* **I decided that I'd
climb on the wall where the cats sit and I'd push your feet
up until somebody came.**

Pause.

27 – APOCALYPTIC LIGHT

*A very low rumble begins. And a light on the floor at the back of the
space comes on. It is industrial, not like the other lights, it starts low
and greenish, but slowly it warms up and become blindingly bright.
Right into the eyes of the audience. It turns TIM and BRYONY into
glowing silhouettes.*

*BRYONY walks around the space slowly taking in all the mess. TIM
watches her.*

*It feels like the aftermath of a disaster of some kind. BRYONY begins
to try and tidy up. She tries to throw the tent back up into the air
but fails and sits down in the wreckage. TIM sits beside her. They
stare at each other.*

Pause.

B: I worry about you all the time. Like what if you get ill
again, really bad…how will we manage, how will I look
after both of you. And I can't help but feel like you are
still hiding and I need you right now Tim.

She lowers her head.

But we can leave it here if you like, they can go. If this is what you want,

She puts her mic down, covers her face. TIM pauses for a moment and then he stands. He removes his rope head, takes the mic stand to centre stage and pauses for a few seconds longer.

28 – TIM'S SPEECH

Delivered very very slowly.

T: Hi I'm Tim.

Pause.

I have chronic depression and acute anxiety.

Pause.

This means that sometimes without my medication I can sink very deep and think about killing myself.

Pause.

But it also means that most of the time I am perfectly happy and I forget it even exists.

Pause.

But do you know what. I have recently begun to become proud of it.

Pause.

See for those eight years I believed that my illness emasculated me. I bought into the idea that feeling sad, crying and doubting the purpose of existence made me LESS of a man, less of a person. I buried my depression so deeply that no one could see it. I used so much of my energy faking it that I just made myself worse. But where did it get me?

Pause.

Over these past year or so I have had to ask myself… why did I do that?

If I had any other illness I would have been on the internet every minute of the day trying to get myself better, but I didn't, I was too ashamed to even type it in.

And I have had to conclude that it has to do with conditioning. That the true version of what it takes to be a real man was not in fact the ideal that I was sold. That any of us were.

Pause.

A real man knows how to speak about his emotions.

A real man shows compassion and integrity.

And a real man understands that there is no such thing as a real man. *(He does inverted commas with his hands.)*

So I agreed to do this show in case it helped people like me. But also because deep down I knew it would help myself. As simple as that sounds, that is why I am here, in this fucking outfit, dancing around on a stage with my mental girlfriend.

BRYONY stands up and starts organising the stage.

I have been told that to tame the beast you have to know the beast. When I first got depression the symptoms were not what I expected them to be and if I can pass one thing on to you it is how to easily identify them, in case they creep up you or someone you know and love. So we made a dance that highlight what they are. I'm still not sure why we couldn't have just listed them. But this is Clinical Depression in its simplest format…with mambo music.

29 – THE SYMPTOMS DANCE

The duo perform the symptoms dance.

They twist and bop in unison to 'Mambo Del Ruletero' by Perez Pardo holding up signs that detail the main symptoms of depression as they go…

Fatigue
Poor Concentration
Worthlessness
Agitation
Achy Bones
Inappropriate Guilt
Indecisiveness
No Appetite
Insomnia
Recurrent Thoughts of Death

TIM heads back to his mic, he is gaining confidence now at public speaking.

30 – TIM'S REPRISE

T: We take the view that we manage my depression together. That we will manage it for the rest of our lives. That we will openly talk about it to our little boy and most importantly that we will never be ashamed of it.

We deal with the disease just like diabetes or asthma. Just like the millions of other people who do exactly the same thing. Tablets or no tablets, politically motivated to change the world or getting on with it behind closed doors.

Mental illness is a fact of life that needs demystifying and de-stigmatising. Our aim with this show is to do our little bit to raise awareness of the fact that suicide is the biggest killer of men under forty-five in the UK…that men are struggling and they need our help.

BRYONY is setting up the guitar, mic, stools and machine in a little cluster in the wreckage of the tent.

I've been told that chronic depression is a life long illness. So I know that at some point in the future I may be ill again. I feel I am only halfway towards understanding my brain and my illness. And there are limits as to how much I can talk about it. And that is frustrating.

Right now I am on a low dose of citalopram to manage my depression. I am in the process of coming off the tablet again, over a much longer period of time. I think it's a good idea

BRYONY joins him at his mic stand.

B: I'm not so sure.

T: She is worried about the baby.

B: He still doesn't talk about lots of things.

T: She is sometimes unhealthily obsessed with my illness.

B: No I just want to be fully prepared.

T: I feel more prepared than I have ever been.

B: Then perhaps we will make another show next year!

T: No chance!

They laugh. She goes and sits on her stool.

To finish I wrote Bryony a song on my guitar. Because I am supposed to be some kind of artist now! It's about the fact that sometimes even now I just want to hide until it all goes away. That sometimes it is hard and not something I feel I can deal with. This is 'The Duvet Song'.

He sings 'The Duvet Song' to BRYONY.

T: *(Singing.)*

I hear the birds celebrate the dawn sun

I hear your words but I feel like I weigh a tonne

I see your eyes welling up. I'm sorry

So I summerise in the code we use…that won't MAKE you worry

Under the duvet

Under the duvet day

I can hear your footsteps arriving home from work

I hope my numbness doesn't drive you too beserk

I hear you flick the faithful kettle on

(B: I love a cup of tea.)

And you lie beside me slurping tea, there's just no question

Under the duvet

It's under duvet day

That's all I can say

It's a cliché, I still whisper as I wait for it to rage

It's an under the duvet

It's an under the duvet day

She kisses him. The lights fade to blackout.

They bow.

The End.

B: Well that was our love story. Sorry gross. But we also recognise that that may be some of your stories too, and if that is the case we like to take this moment at the end of the show to say tonight you have met two fellow members of your tribe. And if you ever wanted to email us then all of our details can be found on your free sheets or at Bryony and Tim dot com. *(She holds up a good luck doll.)* and these little guys were for luck, and we wanted to wish all of you good luck out there, we hope you argue about black socks for the rest of your lives.

Thanks for coming to our show.

by the same author

Credible Likeable Superstar Role Model
9781783190638

WWW.OBERONBOOKS.COM

Follow us on www.twitter.com/@oberonbooks
& www.facebook.com/OberonBooksLondon